SATURN

SATURN

By: Susy Gasca

Illustrations by: Hannah Gelo

*Dedicated to all the pieces of my heart.
You matter.*

Table of Contents

i'd *CUT*

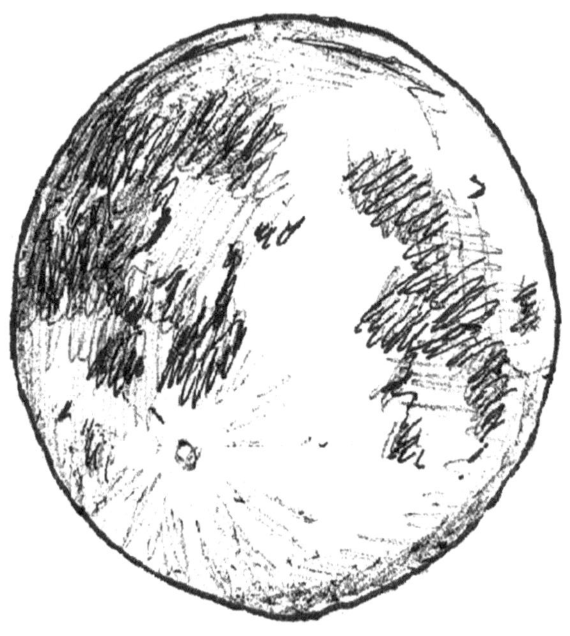

Moon Baby

I stayed looking at the moon,

as I wished upon a star.

that I would have kissed you with more passion

and more love when I had the chance.

How I wished upon a star to keep holding the moon.

My lips gently caressing every inch of your skin.

So fragile and broken you once were.

How I thought you were the moon that would never leave.

I dreamed of you, I and time.

I wished upon a falling star.

You were the star I kept wishing to.

The moon stayed but you left.

A star waits for no one.

Time disappeared after that moment.

I look at the moon and think of you.

The falling star I wished upon.

moonlight

with trembling hands, she held her body still.

to her knees she stumbled.

soft hues of moonlight warming her naked soul.

silent night.

screaming thoughts.

she prayed.

she basked in silence

in the emptiness of the moonlight

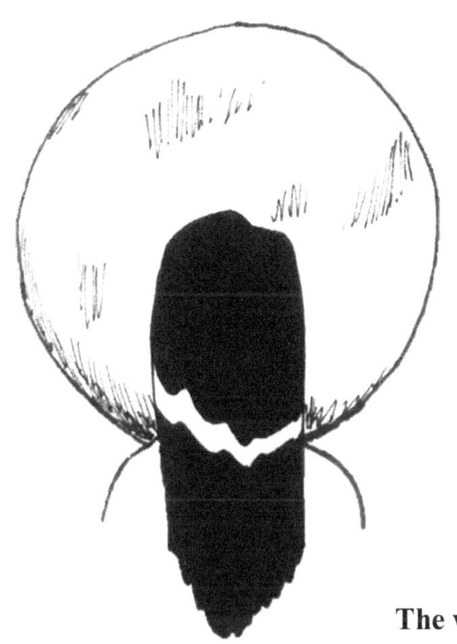

Worthy human.

The world will wake again,

and so will you.

**Your first hug.**

Little birdy.

These visions of peaches are so sweet,

they must have come from Eden.

Spread them, they say.

You open your wings, and they your legs.

There lies the first drafts of becoming a woman.

Stains of white hands, cheap purple eye shadow, and

public education

Cake-thick dirt lines your wings.

Creative entrepreneur, CEO, boss lady.

You can't do that; you are a woman.

Sly and wry, these worms will sliver.

Fly birdy, fly.

After that earthy sugar high.

Jaded, you still dream daily of peaches.

Sweet, bold, daring. You shan't stay still

Inner woman stand, attain your Eden.

To the sweetest of dreams, fly birdy, fly

From her lips to her hips,

purple hues of bruises from the past have no forever

home in the wings meant for flying.

Sweetheart, _this is your second hug._

Embrace your inner galaxies.

A blue moon has passed since I held you close for the

first time.

Ecstasy suffocating me in your embrace.

Darling,

your presence was everything I never knew I wanted.

The moon watched us closely as your breath whispered

love into me.

When my awkward dancing gave me an angel smile,

I fell in love with the universe as it carefully tethered

you and I to exist at once.

I swayed to the rhythm of your laughter,

your hunger,

you.

I came to you from behind and your arms wrapped me

still.

Head against your neck.

You tenderly squeezed your heartbeat all over me.

Your name sloppily yet purposefully etched onto my
existence.

Although you choose another to adore, I sleep at night
knowing I will always choose you.

I held an angel that night. She once held me too

The blue moon watched as I fell more in love with you
than I already knew.

Miss…

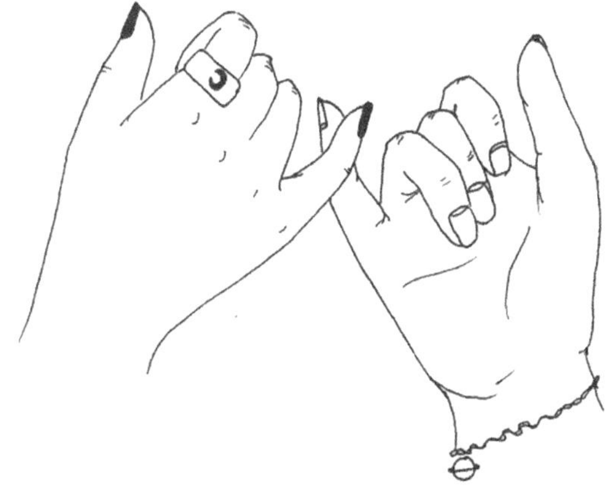

Zombie

Roaming roads that scream pale and ragged.

I forget the vibrancy of painted rocks.

A wilted flower full of pollen,

The streets and I are bare.

Once dead, a dead man continues sleepwalking…

My skin rejoicing in vibrant youth.

A scar-cut-soul lies worn, emotionless, and naked.

I find refuge in the winter chill.

I feel everything and nothing at all.

Pure brown eyes pass by mine softly.

With dull-edged scissors we were parted.

Worlds no longer tethered.

I forget what sunlight feels like.

Living but not alive.

I crave to remember the beat of a heart coming home.

Tired of the fight to stay,

we've become outsiders.

…zombies, not daring to catch each other.

we stay falling.

I don't recognize the yellow lucid sky,

I sleepwalk to numb the pain.

Hands ashen, I drag my feet and lose the day

Convenience

Metallic blood dripping from the thorn,

she watches as rain pours out over crimson red

Stains receding.

Once more,

Time and rain leave me pure.

See it happen as people take charge over you.

Wanting to start again and dance with potential

Reality deems, I am just convenient.

If one matters; time is swept and cleared.

To be seen not just felt.

But once more, their reality screams:

Minutes will pass faster,

I am doing you a favor.

You're on my time,

not sure if you matter.

I've been slit here before,

crimson dripping for months before rainfall.

The damn storm just washed the stains,

I will not shift to the beat of potential

Yes, you matter. I matter too.

Time will hold still, as I sway and dance only

to the tenderness of reality.

I am here.

Piercing eyes and bold strokes.

I was not meant to twist time for your convenience.

White Out

I was plain paper, and I handed you the pen.

You hesitated, then landed your first stroke.

When ink hit paper…

You were poetic

The pen never left the page as you covered every corner.

Traces of the ocean and sunsets graced the medium.

Then pen started wearing,

Freely the pen ran loose.

Ink spilled.

Running blotches danced on paper.

You looked at it and held on for a second.

In a room abounding with empty lined paper,

this was the first time I was tossed.

Yearning for more ink,

I took the white out and started again.

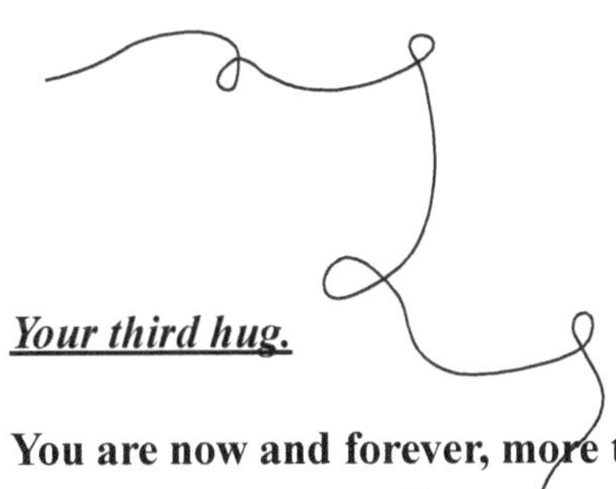

<u>*Your third hug.*</u>

You are now and forever, more than enough.

I pinky promise.

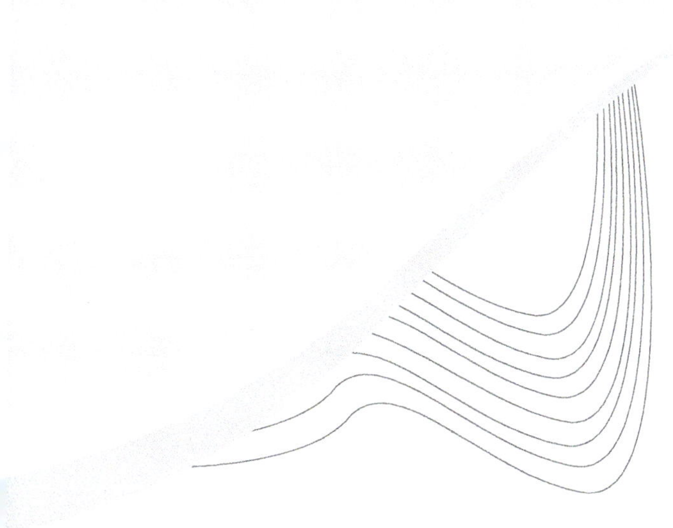

Myself

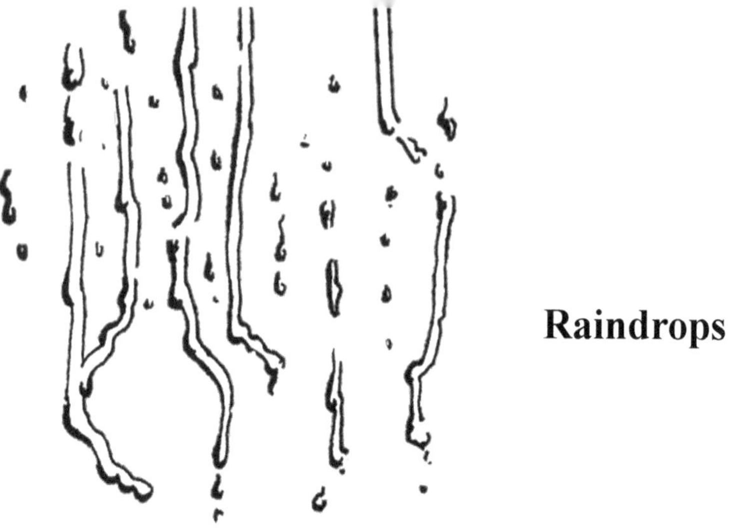

Raindrops

Not much time has passed,

since a cloud of raindrops started dancing against my

windowpane.

I remembered to drop my shoulders to the pitter-patter of

their rhythm.

I'd say it's inexplicable.

My lips painting a slight smile to the fall of rain

An exhale of gratitude for the drops held on the palms of

my hands.

I reach up for more. Just a bit more.

Unknowingly the tears have been running.

Miles far and wide they travel.

From a suburban windowpane to a deserted highway.

Above the clouds,

nestled in the heavens,

they weep.

I'm holding their tears as the angels weep.

Wallflower

Count of fingers for gazes that have met mine.

Treading water on what is my impact.

I'm missing, absent, or anything in between.

A ghost…

… a wallflower longing for touch.

Touch of skin and shoes that I haven't walked in.

How do you become 'existing'?

Dreams of perfect love giving you firsts,

moments where you and life connect.

first dance taken…

grasping onto the shell of my ghost.

his eyes never met mine.

girl he wanted. lie he got.

Soberly, a façade was broken.

Wallflower still longing.

first kiss taken.

Drunkenly she held me. felt me.

…soberly, she gazed past me.

Her mind made up. I was not worth 'existing'

She left me, a ghost.

Crossroads of tired, sad eyes.

Heart stretched out.

Hands weary.

Some say, I'm a human dreamer,

       a silenced and searching soul.

But I say,

       I am a wallflower.

Spineless

she has a disorder you know.

their mayhem spines snatching her confidence.

their jaded lives picking and stealing any form of

worldly existence.

she finds purpose in scarring their cynicism.

she holds their ego front and center.

youthful spirit breaking emotionless people.

powerless, they falter

unable to dim her light.

Her mind as stagnant as still waters,

the world quietly watches.

life being forked into choices,

she stays and steadily washes their feet clean.

powerless, they falter

unable to dim her light

"Why don't you do the same thing back to them? They deserve it."

...because.

What they do is a reflection of them.

What I do is a reflection of me.

Let them be them.

I want to be me.

Half-Assed

a skeleton breathed air well into twenty-one years.

Leash clasped so tight

She exhaled timidly, with reservation

Suppress the flesh, suppress the soul

I don't remember much of the pain.

Skeletons only remember the empty seeping of nothingness.

No life. No sin. No hurt.

Or so you'd think…

Bullshit.

Blood raced as an electric heart was dared into existence.

Buried the chronic liar,

Who'd say, "That's gay, but I'm not".

Cutting past what's ordinary, I don't believe in living a half-

assed existence.

I am enough.

I am gay, and I am enough.

They say:

> You give too much.
>
> …I believe in living to serve.

They say:

> You're too sensitive.
>
> …I will feel my emotions this time.

They say:

> No one will ever love you.
>
> …I will love me.

Skeletons only remember the empty seeping of nothingness

These misunderstood lungs will audaciously breathe this time

IBS

Crouched down,

wave of nausea creeps up in an empty school restroom.

I am repulsive.

Crinkled noses, side-eyed smirks.

Holes in momma's jeans drag heavy with empty pocket

change.

Chipped tooth, broken glasses.

Momma's eyes permanently wrinkle.

I hear the crying, and shaking heads whisper:

"her momma can't fix it"

Ten pounds lighter,

My flesh settles lightly over paper mâché bones.

Relentless, mom prays. I, her walking testimony.

I may be sick and repulsive, but hey at least I won't stay

broken forever.

"what's wrong with me?"

<u>Nothing.</u>

Nothing is wrong with you.

Saturn

Squeezing my heart until it's sucked dry,

I am freezing.

The warmth of your body pressed to mine.

How I ache for you, how I reach for you.

Many say move on,

But they don't see where our hearts have been.

Us escaping the world:

Four hours-in, two coffee cups later.

Traces of your spine, connecting Saturn to the Moon.

Your eyes searching for mine.

I see you. Don't cry. I see you.

We were two kindred spirits looking for healing.

Keep walking. I dared you.

Keep dreaming. I held you.

So beautiful. I loved you.

My blaring chuckle. You gave me.

My brightest smiles. Tied to yours.

My most tragic heartbreak. You.

Standing tall for me when my legs buckled,

In return I pushed your feet.

You walked so far you outgrew me.

Heart squeezed dry.

I am freezing.

And you are warm.

Move on, I say to the heart that's not done protecting.

Live your life unfeigned Saturn. 

Patience my friend.

Their battles look different from yours.

Many people will come to plant a seed, then leave.

Water these seeds and grow.

A select few are worth fighting for.

If you always come back together, maybe just maybe, their roots

have been planted so deep you were meant to be one.

During this time, here lies the grandest of hugs.

to *SAVE*

Petals

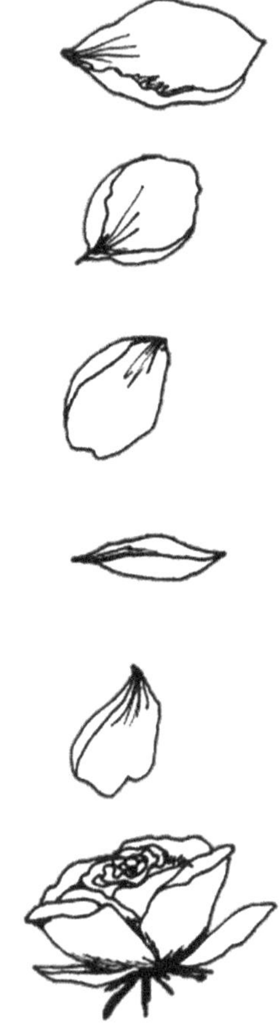

An illusion.

the flower petal drifted to a dark cold underpass.

Unmoved, she searched for sunlight only to fade into

nothingness.

Strong winds swept the petal to a blooming field.

It was there.

With ferocity it held her darkish entangled soul

Harvesting rebirth

the sunlight made her pure

like me. like you. like life.

not all pretty petals stay pretty

not all faded petals stay faded

Unmoved

Glass cage echoes as wobbly steps shuffle

pang pang

Fingerprints stain bare glass door

Souls unable to bypass its guarded lock

pang pang

another soul scratches and fumbles.

Rusted lock stays unmoving.

pang pang

my love seeps, another comes.

Lurching my body I bang against clear glass,

cracks spread with cobwebbed fingers

pang pang

My reflection delicately stares back through the glass

Seconds turn to months

Fingers slowly tracing the cracks

She waits

Lifts a finger and traces my insecurities

My back slumped against razor gripping edges

She doesn't fumble with the battered lock

She taps on the glass cage

Unmoved I stay standing.

Shards of stained glass scatter the floor

Crisp air suddenly dancing with my lungs.

I breathe. The Lord watches as I breathe.

Try as many times as you need darling.

Universe

My fingers slowly trace the universe, and that never

compares to her reality.

She's messy. She's raw. She stumbles. She's flawed.

Her heart beaten and scarred.

I see fire and hunger in her eyes.

Saturn walking with the Moon.

Gravity watches and pulls.

They stretch love apart only to see.

Flames turn to smoke,

Water to ice.

God laughs and interferes.

He says, "against all odds,

this is my universe".

<u>**To all the hers that I love**</u>**, it's quite simple**

…She hasn't just given my life added "humanity".

She's given everyone around her that too.

I pray she sees how truly special she is.

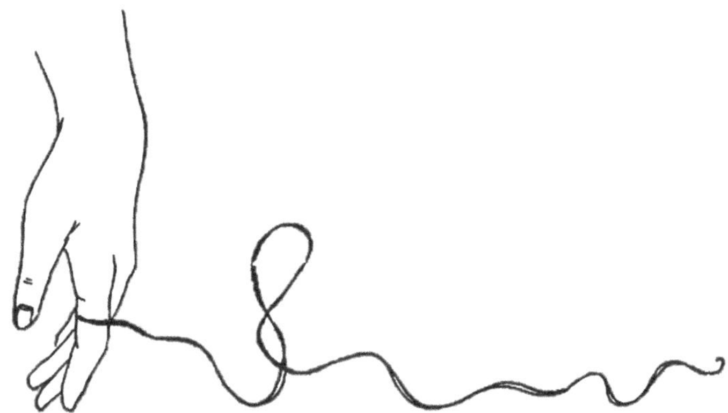

touch

you feel gentle.

clothed in chains

you've wrapped yourself in to feel safe.

obligation rooted in promise,

gently they add more chains

stripped of your peace

you stay stumbling.

reaching for more hearts

you silently beg

love me. don't chain me.

your eyes hold the chains you wish to break.

many have looked through you.

they don't see how you reach for life.

How deeply your roots are embedded in fire-enveloping

faith.

My own chains transparent in front of yours.

I hold your gaze and you plead,

One less chain. Just one.

I nod my head, in silent promise.

Strangers to partners.

The clock stays ticking, and I applaud you.

Benevolently aiding as we strip away sweat-covered

chains

Your new home soon rooted in freedom.

I touch you. You touch me.

We are free.

I love you always.

be free

Exploited

I am not into science.

But why does the world slap hurricanes into our

everyday lives?

…Dismissive.

I let the winds sweep me to my knees.

Debris trapping me into a world of lies, deception, and

pain.

I stay complacent.

They watch as I keep burning in the fire.

Calm as the tides before a storm,

I let the storm pull and push me to its own accord.

Body feeling heavy,

I grow tired.

Used, torn and broken; I've become an object to the rest

of them.

My momma being the most human of us all,

never stooped to becoming the tide flowing with the wind.

She was the wind.

Emerging as worn and raging; I throw compliance to the shore.

Instead, momma watches me stand

and become the whole damn storm.

…Shush your mind gentle overthinker

self-love being your greatest lover mouths out

"You have a home in me."

XoXo

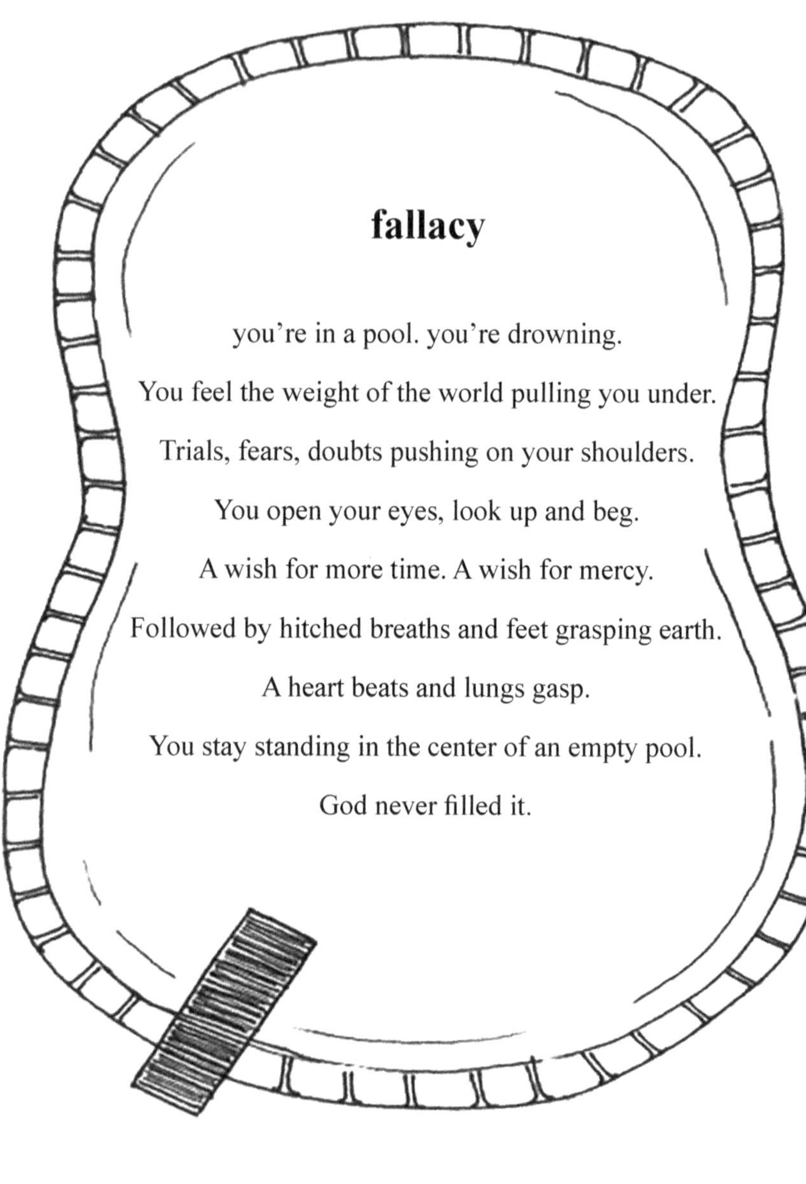

fallacy

you're in a pool. you're drowning.

You feel the weight of the world pulling you under.

Trials, fears, doubts pushing on your shoulders.

You open your eyes, look up and beg.

A wish for more time. A wish for mercy.

Followed by hitched breaths and feet grasping earth.

A heart beats and lungs gasp.

You stay standing in the center of an empty pool.

God never filled it.

Your next hug.

Keep the faith friend.

Society's timeline for my life is not my measure of

success.

Nor should it be yours.

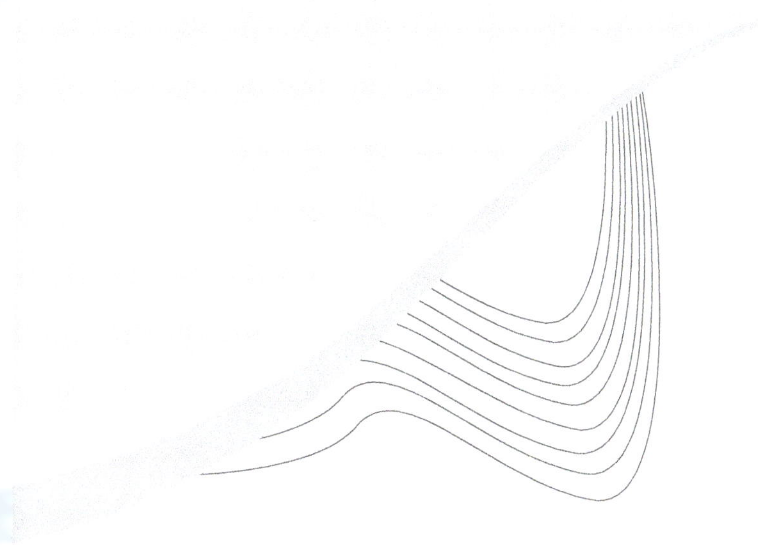

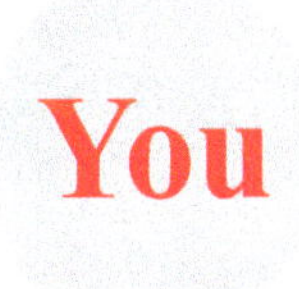

You

If the shoe fits...

As a teen, my first white rose went to a dumb first love.

She never reaches out, but you still do.

It should have been you,

My teddy bear mate.

They picked and poked.

Your grace handed shit back.

To you I always looked up, you stay looking down.

Twirling Jesus on your neck and singing one more song.

You're fourteen, I now close to thirty.

Ruthless, and kind.

You stay forever infinite.

An angel sings, and I hug you tighter.

My fingers fumble with the purest of white roses.

Gently laying it on the bed of your cancer.

Here's to taking your pain, I hope someday mine too.

Friends deserve white roses. It's true.

The earth's lifelong hug to you.

In all the sun's golden light.

Breathe...

Drive fast, hands out.

Feel that? The wind rushing against your fingertips.

Look at you. You're catching time.

Sister

The womb that first held my heart held yours too.

As much as you may fight it,

my heart will always be tied to yours.

your first steps,

your wavering choices,

your unanswered questions.

I pray you won't ever feel forgotten.

The strings holding my heart together have the answers

to your questions.

Because you too have seen my first steps in life,

my wavering choices,

my unanswered questions.

Your heart is never lonely.

Your heart was formed tied to mine.

Destiny will always intertwine our human existence.

You will never be forgotten,

So bright-eyed, so beautiful you are.

Garden

rows of flowers stood lively

boasting with gusto

few stood weathered.

    Tussled roughly, built with tougher edges.

    A sprinkle of superficial beauty.

    snapped branches, burnt edges

    I chose these.

these were my people

    snapped branches, burnt edges

    my heartbeat ran with them

        fast and far it went.

            broken down cars.

            summer's brain fog.

            forehead kisses.

            fractured dreams.

waking mistakes.

snapped branches, burnt edges

they bled life into me.

I chose these flowers and watered them

Roots emerging

Our existence flowed as we breathed life together.

Scars, tribulations, and brokenness watered to life

We chose to exist together,

In a garden overflowing with gusto and superficial

beauty

I'll choose them this life to the next

snapped branches, burnt edges

this is my garden

Blue Jeans

He stole my girl…

Anchored her soul, dreams, and smile to the loops of his jeans.

Cut and tailored,

He stripped the material that didn't fit.

He likes them form fitted.

So tight he can barely breathe.

She exhales enough oxygen to fill his searching lungs.

She's eccentric and alive

A fire light set ablaze in the water.

He likes her colors.

But she's not meant to fit in.

She's different.

He looks for familiarity in a pair of old blue jeans

He grabs some scissors and cuts.

"This will not do"

He cuts and sews

He walks, she follows.

Sewn into the loops of his jeans,

He's stolen my girl.

The one whose imperfections are perfect,

And whose energy is free.

Cut and sew. Cut and sew.

He continues to strip her of all she owns.

But man, oh man

You don't know her.

You can strip her of all she owns,

but you will never strip her of all that she is.

She's magic.

Bright, brilliant, and bold she glows

…she will never be your pair of old worn blue jeans

Precious soul, you are worth more than graceless

hands that have touched your body without caressing

the scars.

You are infinitely limitless.

Love You Baby

Momma told me, "I love you baby".

In return, I pulled out of my pocket:

Love, passion, and a whole lot of God.

Watch me walk momma.

I'm gonna show them my heart.

The world won't stop it from beating.

Just watch me walk momma.

Just watch me walk.

Some reassurance for your searching heart.

Her: "I think when someone falls in love with you, you'll be easy to love."

Me: Why?

Her: "…because you're easy to smile and easy to laugh."

You are.

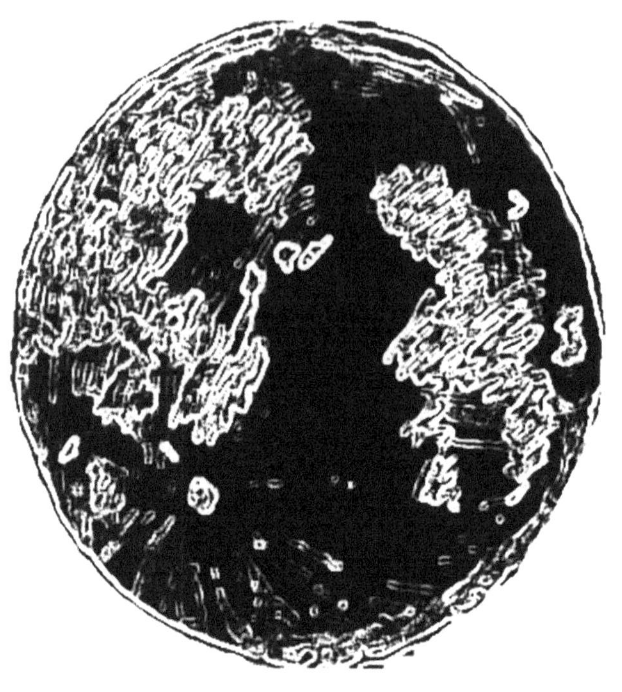

New Moon

I tried to forget your warmth.

      Your white blanket hue painted in the night.

When you disappeared, I closed my eyes.

You were the falling star I wished upon.

And falling stars don't come back.

Months later, my stitched heart still felt the

whispers of your light in my soul.

I opened my eyes, and the star was still gone.

But you were here.

In my arms.

      In my heart.

            In the night sky.

                  You were here.

With more miles and scars than I remembered,

You were farther and dim.

So scattered and drained,

I tried to breathe life into your lungs.

You hid.

But I remembered you.

 I remember that hue,

  And your white blanket warmth.

Hi New Moon. I see you.

You are there. In the bare night sky.

You were always there.

I look at the moon and think of you.

The piece of my heart I forever love.

You're hurting again moon babe.

How I pray you live, love and dance in the moonlight

once more.

I look at the sky and wish upon you.

To new beginnings, my new moon.

I'd Cut Myself to Save You

(& I don't regret it)

Continue to dream with your eyes open,

always.

from my garden to yours

much love,

Suz

Letter from the Author...

Hi there sunshines, Susy here. I would like to thank you for allowing me the opportunity to share my self-love project with you.

You don't know how far you can go unless you try.

If this book has reached your hands, the trying was worth the fight. Here's to more self-love, kindness, boldness and hugs (lots of them). I'm rooting for you all the way.

Here's a little word vomit about me, from me. I am a fellow human, friend, and dreamer. I grew up in a conservative Christian household and I am proudly a part of the LGBTQ+ community. We all rock! As a somewhat young adult, I am still learning what it means to heal from a lack of self-love. That is more than okay as healing is meant to be a continuous journey. You may catch me in Arizona: out with family and friends, hiking, jogging, off-roading in my jeep (her name is Ganzo), or volunteering at a non-profit. A dream of mine is to make a positive difference with a non-profit of my own within my lifetime. I'm also a bit of an introvert so if I'm not doing any of that, I tend to be on my own. To date, I work a full-time nursing position and get to help some lovely patients. I also get to tell them cheesy jokes… but I suppose that's enough about me. Now it's your turn. I dare you to write your story. I'd be honored to read it.

Thank you for your presence and existence.

Keep dreaming, striving, and living. It's worth it, it is.

-Saturn